PROBLEM SOLVING

Solve Any Problem Like a Trained Consultant.

Peter Oliver

PROBLEM SOLVING

Copyright © 2018 by Concise Reads™

All rights reserved. No part of this publication may be reproduced in any form or by any means without the prior written permission of the publisher or author.

DISCLAIMER: The author's books are only meant to provide the reader with the basic knowledge of a certain topic, without any warranties regarding whether the reader will, or will not, be able to incorporate and apply all the information provided. Although the author and publisher have made every effort to ensure that the information in this book was correct at press time, the author and publisher do not assume and hereby disclaim any liability to any party for any loss, damage, or disruption caused by errors or omissions, whether such errors or omissions result from negligence, accident, or any other cause.

TABLE OF CONTENTS

1. INTRODUCTION

2. DEFINING THE PROBLEM

3. STRUCTURING THE PROBLEM

4. PROJECT MANAGEMENT

5. FINAL SYNTHESIS

INTRODUCTION

If you are or aspire to become a business executive then you cannot escape being confronted with problem solving situations from internal operations to external customer facing decisions. <u>Problem solving is a learned skill.</u> As such, you have to learn the right way to do it, then you have to practice in every problem you face. If you don't learn the skill, you might find yourself hitting a self-imposed corporate ceiling.

Problem solving is not only a skill important for the corporate world. It is vital for companies in the startup phase of their lifecycle. If you're in that group, then you have undoubtedly seen many titles on 'product innovation' or 'business model innovation' among others that will supposedly fuel your idea generation. They may, but I've never bought these books. I like to focus on the principles.

The principle foundation of innovation is a strong skill in problem solving.

The principle foundation of creative thinking is a strong skill in problem solving.

There are many forms that problem solving can take and here I want to share the top three most common forms differentiated by how much time you have to apply the principles:

1. **On-the-spot problem solving (short-term):** In this case, your problem solving ability becomes analogous to effectively communicating your thoughts. If you can't problem solve

correctly, then think of that as having the same effect as when you forget your speech during a presentation. That's how important this skill is if you are or are planning on becoming a business executive. The business executives who never get promoted are the ones who listen to an employee bring up several ideas or issues and then look at their assistant and say "Tom, what do you think of all this?". Everyone can see that person does not have problem solving skills---it is very obvious. Subordinates get discouraged from bringing problems to their boss, and those weak in problem solving are just avoided like the plague. In the business world, it's a poor quality not to be able to think on your feet. In fact, thinking on your feet is not really as spontaneous as people think but the result of continued practice of the principles of problem solving.

2. **Looming deadline problem solving (intermediate-term):** In this case, you have a few days or weeks to problem solve. Your best tool is prioritization. You'll need to decide which problems or issues need to be solved first to help solve the subsequent issue or problem. How well you do with prioritization will mean the difference between delivering on time or coming up short.

3. **Goal oriented problem solving (long-term):** In this case, you do not need to solve the problem today, but you do need to have a process in place

so you could come back to the problem when new information or updates become available. Because you have all the time in the world, prioritization is not front and center. Instead, your attention should be focused on building a robust <u>work plan</u> with regular revisiting of the original problem.

Looking at a problem in terms of its **time dimension** is the first step in thinking of a problem. In the rest of this concise read, we'll learn how to structure a problem based on the information and context presented to us. This should be fun, so let's get started.

For the purposes of teaching you the skill of problem solving, we will look at it the way consultants from different industries look at a problem.

Step 1: Define the problem: use timing and character then clearly articulate the question that we need to answer. If you've ever worked with a trained consultant you'll watch them listen respectfully to a problem being described and then after everyone is done talking, they would start with "so what I'm hearing is that …" and then proceed to describe the problem using problem solving principles!

Early in my career , it made me feel dumb when others had to rephrase my description of a problem. However, it was exactly what I needed to be convinced that problem solving was a simple skill I was determined to acquire.

Step 2: Structure the problem: Here we'll use Mckinsey's famous MECE framework or mutually exclusive but collectively exhaustive framework as well as a borrowed concept from data science known as decision and issue trees.

Step 3: Process the problem: We'll use Pareto's principle and answer our problem questions within the deadline.

Step 4: Articulate the solution: In this last step, correct communication is of utmost importance. You may have solved the problem, and all you are missing is taking the insight generated and making them <u>actionable</u>. People who fail step 4 get the very common response of "so what?". Some people are nicer though and assume you don't have the capacity to complete step 4 and just thank you for the information and they go on to complete step 4 and ultimately receive top billing with a minor credit line for your efforts. Step 4 is easy--it just has to be practiced.

DEFINING THE PROBLEM

We've learned to first factor in the TIMING of a problem. We then have to factor in the CHARACTER of the problem. Defining the character of a problem helps structure your thinking of the solution.

Experts define a problem with up to 4 characteristics:

1. Analytical/quantitative
2. Conceptual/creative problem.
3. Divergent
4. Convergent

Remember that nothing in life is fixed, and as a general rule this applies here. A problem can have multiple characteristics. For example, if you are tasked with figuring out the right target audience and marketing campaign for a new SaaS product. This problem has an analytical component because you have to figure out the most <u>profitable</u> segment that also <u>will want</u> to buy your product. You'll have to look at past sales and other historical data to come up with that answer. Additionally, this same problem has a creative or conceptual component because you have to find the right message to appeal to that audience otherwise all the analytical work in identifying the right business model and right audience would be for nothing.

Additionally, we could be given one piece of information and asked to generate lots of ideas in which case we would characterize the problem as **divergent** problem. On the other hand, if we are given lots of pieces of information and we only want one solution, then we are faced with a **convergent** problem.

But why do we have to factor in the TIMING and CHARACTER of a problem? You'll see that this is a fundamental way of breaking a problem into clear questions that need to be answered to solve the problem. If this doesn't make sense yet, keep reading and keep practicing--after all, insight without action is just insight, not a skill.

Timing and character definitions of the problem should be quick mental deductions just to orient your thinking. Once you solve multiple problems with these mental constructs, you will eventually start seeing patterns that work for you when solving analytical vs. creative problems or divergent vs. convergent problems. The mental constructs are just mental indexing for future problems. The real meat and powerful next step is reaching close to 100% problem definition.

Problem Definition: After defining the type of problem, we need some more information to achieve 100% problem definition. This is where you should ask important questions to gather the most information. Important questions that **define** the problem are related to:

A. Context
B. Scope of the problem
C. Stakeholder analysis
D. Constraint analysis.

You MUST know which <u>stakeholders</u> are affected by the problem so you do not forget to factor them into your solution. You MUST know what the <u>constraints</u> are so you don't even consider solutions that are not feasible, out of budget, or just unrealistic given the resources available.

Some business schools teach the **SMART** acronym when generating problem questions to define the problem. This stands for:

S: Specific (think character)

M: Measurable (think character)

A: Actionable

R: Relevant (think context and scope)

T: Time bound (think timing)

The SMART acronym is a good framework to define the problem. With time you will see that you will have created mental heuristics or shortcuts that work for you. I started out with SMART but then quickly moved to identifying the timing, character, then the context and scope to rephrase the problem into an actionable question. It's the same end result but a faster deconstruction for me.

What if we don't have 100% problem definition? This happens frequently when we are asked to problem solve on the spot. In these situations we may never reach 100% problem definition, and it therefore becomes imperative to make our assumptions explicit. This is an exercise of <u>explicitly stating our assumptions</u> to fill in the problem definition. The reason for that is by doing so in an explicit way we challenge our assumptions and we can think of them in the form of probabilities. You will see that if you list your four assumptions to fill in the problem definition, you will find that you are only pretty sure about three and that the fourth one is more a guess than an educated assumption. So you focus on three assumptions to define the problem and make a mental note to pressure test the fourth assumption to see if the problem definition can be improved.

STRUCTURING THE PROBLEM

After defining the problem, the next step is structuring the problem and prioritizing deliverables. When we are given a few days or even a week to solve a problem, we find that there are many tasks that need to be done from consulting experts to gathering necessary documentation from collaborators and engaging with stakeholders.

These short bursts of problem solving are very common in the private equity and venture capital industry--what is often referred to as due diligence prior to acquisition or investment. Given a limited amount of time, we are offered the opportunity to do an in-depth analysis, but we often find that there is never enough time. That is why prioritization is important.

Ask yourself what are the three most important insights that would lead me to my goal--in the case of private equity, what are the three most important insights that would push our team to invest or to skip on a potential acquisition. The next problem we find with these one week problem solving sessions is that one insight begets even more questions, so approaching the problem in a structured way allows us to know how far we want to go down the rabbit hole and when we should stop and move on.

Let's keep it concise shall we? The steps to structuring the problem for a short-term project such as a due diligence study are as follows:

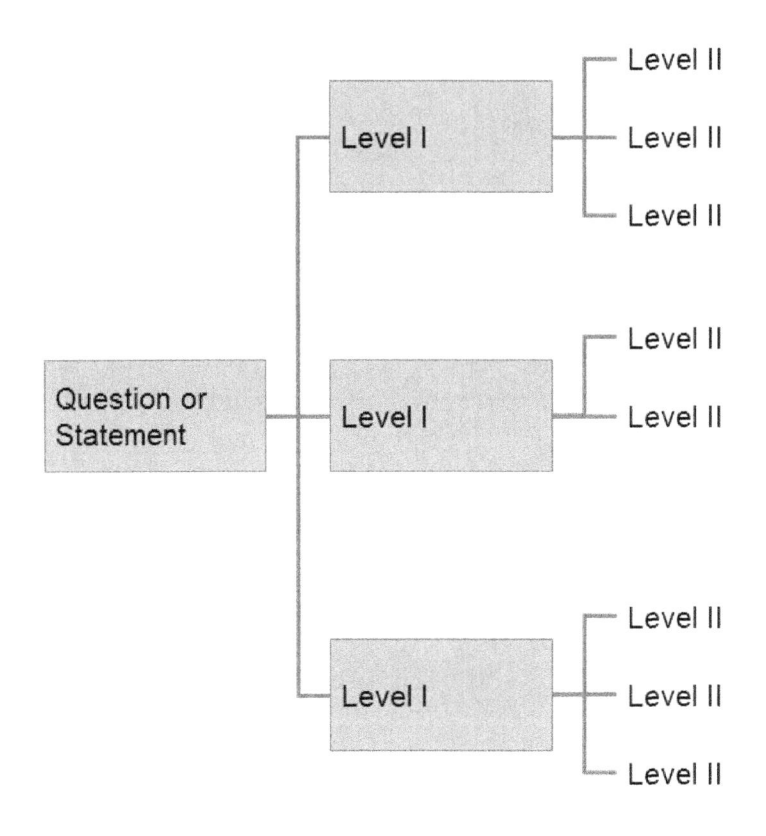

1. **Define the Problem**
2. **Structure the problem into its component parts**

Here, the intended goal is to reach components that are <u>MECE</u> or mutually exclusive and collectively exhaustive. That way we are sure we won't miss anything, and when we assign work to different members of a team--we know that their work won't overlap. Note that this is the intended goal, and most times the final output won't be 100% MECE.

Once you've reached a point where tasks can be divided and analysis can begin, don't waste more time trying to achieve a perfect MECE chart.

To develop this MECE chart we use a common problem solving technique known as logic trees of which we have two subtypes. An **issue tree** begins with a **question** on the left hand side and then is broken into level 1 components using the question **"How?"**.

These are then broken into level II components using the same "**How?**" question. Issue trees are most commonly used when we have all the facts and it is a matter of breaking it down to all its components.

On the other hand, if we don't have all the facts, or there are too many facts, or we have the availability of a subject matter expert on the team, then we would use a **hypothesis tree** instead. A hypothesis tree starts with a **statement** on the left hand side and each level is broken up using the question '**Why?**''. When we've structured our problem into components, we then analyze the final components and see if they are insightful and can lead to actions such as a specific analysis or direct us to interview stakeholders or external experts to answer the component or branch of the tree in question.

On occasion, the final components either make no sense at the onset, or after investigation yield little to no results. At that point, despite structuring the problem, the problem is left unanswered. In this case, we have another tool to help us out. We use three common techniques used by academics to restructure our problem.

- **Point of view analysis**: we look at the problem from the lens of a competitor or a stakeholder and break down the components from that perspective.

- **Assumption reversal**: we reverse some or all of our initial assumptions (since they didn't yield any results in the first run). For example, let's assume our problem is to find out why a company is unprofitable. We assume it must be in their operations because the market demand is there, but then find out there is nothing wrong with their operations. If we reverse our assumption that market demand is high, and begin breaking it down, we might find that demand is high for a bundled product and the company we are investigating only offers an unbundled product. Simple, but powerful.

- **Constraint release:** We initially set constraints in our <u>definition of the problem</u>. If our structuring of the problem does not yield results, then we need to relax some of those constraints and restructure the problem.

3. **Prioritization:** This last step is subjective based on the goal of the project. In IT projects, usually three metrics used for prioritization are cost, risk, and feasibility. In private equity due diligence studies, we look at impact and feasibility. Impact here typically means how much of the problem can we answer by doing the analysis for this one component. In general, and I've spoken on this before--the **80/20 Pareto principle** is applied where we assume that 20% of the components will yield 80% of the result. Of Course that's not exact science, but there have to be more impactful components in order for us to be able to prioritize our time. Feasibility is another important factor because while we might like to get a complete answer, sometimes our

answer will likely fall short because of inadequate resources. Lastly, for prioritization to work, we need to understand if we are converging or diverging towards an answer. By that I mean, are we choosing the terminal branches of an issue tree that will converge to a single answer, or are we picking branches that are far apart from each other to produce multiple answers. Keep that in mind so that you don't pick terminal branches that lead you to one answer when the client or your boss wanted a divergent view.

** This section is purposely concise so your time is not wasted. However, I encourage you to read it once more. There is a lot of information, and you need to try it out once for yourself in a real life problem to see how you move from a problem statement (i.e. defining the problem) to breaking the problem into unanswered How's or Why's and prioritizing which branches to answer first using the Pareto principle so you could meet the deadline.

PROJECT MANAGEMENT

For longer term projects, the type that requires a large investment from the firm and requires a future vision of the product months or years in advance, the approach is slightly more complex.

We continue to practice what we learned earlier such as setting up a SMART problem definition, structuring our problem into its MECE components and prioritizing on the tasks with the highest impact for the company.

For a large project you'll find that you have multiple different issues that are prioritized. Before jumping in and firing on all cylinders, this is where the manager will need to pause and create what's known as a **work plan**. In short, it is deciding on the resources and deadlines for all priority branches ahead of time.

The **work plan** takes the prioritized issues from our issue tree or what we'll call the 'what' and decides on the 'how' and the 'when'. The biggest benefit of a work plan is that it optimizes for **interdependencies** and **sequencing**.

Interdependencies between work streams is common in project management, and that should be taken into account when deciding which workstream to start first in order to feed into another prioritized workstream to avoid <u>overlapping</u> <u>work</u> or worse repeating the same processes.

Sequencing of the workstreams is ordering the work streams from the point of view of limited resources. You could have 3 out of 5 issues that require a data scientist, but you only have 2 data scientists and you know that 1 of the workstreams is twice as long as the other two. In that situation, optimized sequencing means assigning a data scientist to each of the shorter tasks, and then assigning both to the third task. To connect this concept with interdepencies, if the third task has interdepencies with other workstreams, then an optimized work plan will place 2 data scientists in the longer third workstream first.

Start with interdependencies then use sequencing for proper resource allocation.

**Note: Included in the workplan is targeted points in the progress of the project to get buy-in from stakeholders. When to engage with different stakeholders should be planned ahead of time to coordinate the workstreams that need to be completed to get to the next phase of the project. In a simple example is that of a startup looking for funding and partnerships. Do they ask for funding after an MVP? Do they need funding to reach an MVP? At which point in the dev cycle do they engage stakeholders including future clients? This all goes into the workplan.

Let's talk about the how and when components go into a work plan. If you google **'work plan worksheet'** you'll get a number of different ways of organizing your project. I'll offer a common simple one used by the Fortune 500 organizations. Each row in this example is known as a workstream or product. In an excel sheet, create the following columns:

1. **Issue:** These are the prioritized issues or the terminal branches of your issue tree. This starts the process of building your workplan for the next few months or even years.

2. **Hypothesis:** This is your best guess answer to the questions in the issue tree

3. **Assumptions:** These are the assumptions you used to come up with your hypothesis

4. **Analyses:** These are the analyses required to prove those assumptions. This is where the bulk of the time is spent and includes expert interviews

and data analyses. Deciding on the right type of analyses is important as one analysis can bring you closer to proving your assumptions than another and here also we prioritize to use the most impactful analyses.

5. **Sources:** this the data or resources you'll need to accomplish the analyses. Using the wrong source is one of the most common errors in analyses.

6. **Owner:** the workstream or product owner is responsible to prove or disprove the hypothesis and is the one responsible for meeting the deadline. Accountability, including a public display of the workplan goes a long way to meet deadlines.

7. **Deadline:** Everything has to have a deadline to set the pace, however keep in mind interdependencies and sequencing and fill this out last.

Once you've set up the work plan in excel (or google sheets) or another tool that can be shared with the different product owners, you should set up a process to periodically revise the workplan. Revise? Yes! It turns out the workplan is always a work in progress. It's a dynamic document maintained by the project leader or manager so it needs to be revisited often.

New resources could become available that completely alter syndication or one of the workplans could be delayed which will delay its interdependencies down the line, and so keeping an eye on the long-term and an eye on the short-term, it behooves the manager to update the workplan <u>at least every 2 weeks</u> if not weekly. Sometimes, there may be no changes made, but the onus is on the manager to mitigate future risk of failure whether it is failure of analyses, or failure to meet the deadline.

FINAL SYNTHESIS

Synthesis is not summarizing.

After you've put in all this hard work to solve a problem, if you present your findings as a summary, it will take away significantly from the work you did. Being able to synthesize your findings allows the manager be looked at as more of a leader and someone who is thinking beyond the problem and more into how it affects the company as a whole.

Synthesis is broken down into insights and implications. Let's use a fun example!

Let's assume you were tasked to find out how to increase revenue by selling baby shampoo. You find out that the largest target consumer are young mothers. You hypothesized that they would prefer a large gallon size bottle and proved your hypothesis through a focus group test followed by an initial sample run. If you present to your leadership the following "We think the best way to increase revenue is by selling gallon size baby shampoo bottles to young mothers" you will surely look ill prepared. Before reading the next paragraph, re-read that summary and convince yourself that this is a summary and not something worthy of a trained problem solver.

First you need to derive insight from your finding. If the finding was an assumption backed by data, then you need to divide that branch into additional branches.

Why do young mothers prefer gallon shampoo bottles? Is it because of cost or convenience? If it is because of cost, then the implication is different than if it were for convenience.

Let's play out the scenario.

If young mothers prefer gallon size baby shampoo bottles because of cost, then instead of retooling manufacturing which is an added cost, it may be more cost effective to offer bulk sales. On the other hand, if it is because of convenience and limiting the number of trips to the store, then offering online shopping and investing in distribution will increase revenues. Insights and implications together make up a synthesized recommendation.

This section could have not been written if it was not for the countless times I've seen ambitious managers fail to showcase their leadership potential. As a rule, never present summaries, only synthesized recommendations. Otherwise, you're asking the leadership to come up with the 'so what?' after your presentation, which means you are not included in the executive level decisions, and you are only as good as the summary results. Simple lesson, but it makes a big difference in how you are perceived in terms of ability and potential.

Now that you've learned the steps to problem solving, it's time to take these lessons into practice so you can learn the nuances of actual experience versus learning. It's also useful to test some of the problem solving technique in conversation. Next time someone rambles on for 5 minutes, take what they've said and break it up into its components then restate the problem. You won't sound annoying, rather if you do it with a smile, you'll sound like you were actively listening and synthesizing the information. Also, never put your hand out in order to stop the other person from talking so you could rephrase the problem. That just shows you are impatient. Practice active listening, THEN define the problem.

Good luck, and pick up your next copy of Concise Reads to acquire new lessons and skills in business.

Also if there is a topic you are interested in, send us an email and get in touch. We appreciate primary market research and will happily produce a new Concise Reads to meet the demand.

--The End--

Printed in Great Britain
by Amazon